Pythagorean Silence

Susan Howe

For Sharon
from Susan Howe

THE MONTEMORA FOUNDATION INC.
Box 336 Cooper Station
New York, N.Y.
10276

Some of these poems first appeared in *Contact II, Credences,
New World Journal, Sulfur* and *Telephone*.

Pythagorean Silence has been published as a special supple-
ment to *Montemora*, a journal of international poetry and
poetics, with support from NEA, CCLM and NYSCA.

The Montemora Foundation, Inc. is a non-profit, tax-exempt
corporation devoted to international poetry and sponsored by
donations and the sale of its publications.

Cover by Judy Fendelman.

we that were wood

when that a wide wood was

In a physical Universe playing with

words

Bark be my limbs my hair be leaf

Bride be my bow my lyre my quiver

I

Pearl Harbor

Buffalo

12.7.41

(Late afternoon light.)

(Going to meet him in snow.)

   HE

     (Comes through the hall door.)

The research of scholars, lawyers, investigators, judges
Demands!

   SHE

     (With her arms around his neck
     whispers.)

Herod had all the little children murdered!

It is dark
The floor is ice

they stand on the edge of a hole singing—

In Rama
Rachel weeping for her children

refuses
to be comforted

because they *are* not.

R

(her cry

silences

whole

vocabularies

of *names*

for

things

(and TALKATIVE
says we are all in Hell.)

GHOST enters   WAVES   he

scatters flowers

from the summit

of a cliff that beckons on or beetles o'er

his base

                    ORISONS

                wicket-gate
                wicket-gate

                        MAGPIES clatter

            1   2   3

                        and TALKATIVE
            (Walks all this time by himself saying
            he says to me softly—)

            What.

                         sway in cauled forgetfulness
                              GATEWAY
                         and setting free
LAW the laws
                    broken
                    to be obeyed

soon forgotten—
moves home again—
is herself again—

Leaning in enclitic ne
                              I cannot
call presence and in its
                              absence
                                        fold in one hand
                         what
     a few
              fragments   holds us to
                                             what

Hear earth born old
hush

no name or mane   but nick
in time

and clock
a foil for future

marching
Marching

to Pale
with face for fool

thrumming
'Hollow hollow holds all'

Faintly the scene is played
softly

snow spread on sound

skip pebbles in secret also

drawn and drawn together
mirrors thaw

only   Only
what never stops hurting remains

in memory

In memory
Errant turns to

and away

Farewel—
twin half torn to pearl

not a sparrow

shall fall

Spires cast long shadows

clouds pass

and sink into prayer on a spire

Buffalo roam in herds
up the broad streets connected by boulevards

and fences

their eyes are ancient and a thousand years
too old

hear murder throng their muting

Old as time in the center of a room
doubt is spun

and measured

Throned wrath
I know your worth

a chain of parks encircles the city

Snow coming and beauty of long shadows tumbling
down
down
on every oak   pine   juniper   beech   birch
and other sweet wood   (holly)

My bones are buffalo and shake their manes

like chaff before earth

lasting to everlasting

for floods have lifted up their waves

heaven and evening are running on the sand
together

invisible and peace come spilling   softly

like snow

February seems
stable

clarity of frozen   Chance

veiled as ever   February ends

will go north through woods to the wood   hoo
to call

what name?

Abstractions of the world's abstraction
warm my icy feet

Who is   my shepherd
invisible

and outside
shape (sheep) impossible hope

by the still waters

Ah invisible

set nimble clocks at every station

constellations of duration

The stress of meaning
dances

in an empty place with clowns
in crowns

sorrows are sectors
with actors

Running   Tell the running

at rest
or in motion

Chance will shove you

shade or shine

Space steps into breath
Breadth into will

will into target (trees)

targets are tender trees

Forever and for
ever

winds away   Look

back
Innermost

Broods infinity boundless

Dithyrambs
into axioms   accurate

as air (refraction) water
(reflection)

Transcendent could be whis

buried

Or as snow fallen

Could be cold snow
falling

Lie down in snow

Do nothing
wrong

but Wrong

A sea beast sunning alone

in still
shared secrets of the sea

the Open

power of vision   a vast
zero

or zest for action

an idea   an Ideal

shrugged into shade
or shoal

Once again

is erratic   will

morning star evening star will
rise

and swim   and sink again
Slipping

forever

between rupture and rapture

soul
severed from Soul   drowned

Drowned

Mother and father
turn downward your face

peace in the basement

all the dogs chained

Shadows are seated at the kitchen table
Clock

and shadow of a Clock

A black cloud hangs over the landscape
War

some war—

Only the fist of fame passing   degrees
of wilderness

of cause   it is the cause

The doors of the fortress are open

engaged couples
buried in epochs of armor

exhibit themselves

They had hoped to prolong human life
by several centuries

but did not live to do so

Their words are weeds wrapped round my head

Roses have withered—it crows rigidly dark

Body and Soul
will we ever leave childhood together

II

*Pythagorean
Silence*

He plodded away through drifts of i

ce

away into inapprehensible Peace

A portable altar strapped on his back

pure and severe

A portable altar strapped on his back

pure and severe

In the forests of Germany he will feed

on aromatic grass and browse in leaves

1.

age of earth and us all chattering

a sentence   or character
suddenly

steps out to seek for truth   fails
falls

into a stream of ink   Sequence
trails off

must go on

waving fables and faces   War
doings of the war

manoeuvering between points
between

any two points   which is
what we want   (issues at stake)

bearings and so

holes in a cloud   are minutes passing
which is

which
view   odds of images swept rag-tag

silver and grey
epitomes

seconds   forgeries engender
(are blue)   or blacker

flocks of words flying together   tense
as an order

cast off to crows

2.

cataclysmic Pythagoras   Things
not as they are

for they are not   but as they seem
(as mirror

in mirror to be)

Sow bare grain   it may chance
of wheet

Wheel of mutable time   Fortune fabled
to turn

(known circumference attached to a frame)
Thoughts are born

posthumously

Dark as theology's secret book
the unsphered stars

are touchstones at a gallop   Dark
irrevocably dark

(written on a stray sheet) years ago
and the chained beast

stamping
But I am wandering off into irrational

magnitudes

Earth has turned away from the sun
and it is night

(Seventy lines about fields in the dark)

so dark seems pleasant land
so dark seems national

3.

earliest before sunrise   Last
before sunset

twilight   (between day
and dark)

is about to begin   And with time
I could do it

ends childhood
Time an old bald thing   a servant

(Do this

or that) Time's theme
And so we go on through the deeps of

childhood (afterglow of light on trees)
Daybreak

by dying
has been revealed   Midday or morrow

move motherless

(Oh women women look) how my words
flow out

kindling and stumbling   Sunwise
with swords and heys

a dance of disguise
where breath most breathes   (Books

blaze up
my room is bright) World I have made

empty edge
Father's house forever falling

Catch and sketch the chilly evening

4.

no more a long future   the present
(shelter)   mosses

shade
and violets prim   are torn

from life
by Love   my Oblivion soaring above

tears the theme away

Superstructures of allegory have been

raised
There is a storm at sea

someone seems to die   Blind love
is eyeless

An eyeless king (cloak worn to rags)
moves

backwards and forwards   from reef
to reef   Lost

to grief   How lust
(these were the ghost's words) crawls

between heaven and earth

Dust is birth
of earth we make loam   substance

and strange shadows

But I am reaching the end   Sky
melts away into sand

sand into Sound   (shelter so loved
by its owner)

Lie down and stray no farther (Sweet
evening

quiet thoughts)

blind love and beginning of dark woods

5.

I thought I did not live in night

for the future   I used to say
lighting the light

farewell to star   and star
As if light spreading

from some sounding center   might
measure even how

familiar
in the forest   losing the trees

Shadows   only shadows
met my gaze   Mediator

I lay down and conceived   Love
(my dear Imaginary)   Maze-believer

I remember   you were called
sure-footed

and yet off the path   (Where
are you) warmed and warming   Body

turned and turning   Soul
identical soul   abandoned

to Sleep   (where
are you crying)

crying for a mother's help   (fell

forests or plant forests)   Dreams
wheel their pale course

We write in sand
three thousand proverbs and songs

bottom is there   but depth
conceals it   Dreams wander

through the body of a parent
Rub hands together   stressing how

we are made of earth   inevitable
our death   Wisdom

a sorry thing   dream in a Dream
remembering a dream

mimic presentation stained with mortality

6.

Number of an acre   and acre
are the same

army is the number of an army

Who knows

what number in number   alone
stands heretic

if one is not   What
will follow

Guardians of law
in the evening of life lay down

the law
(Plato had a thin voice) clearly

in *Laws* that man is a puppet

(Socrates was a midwife
but this is secret)

Words are not acts
out of my text I am not what I play

When I went to bed I seemed to be
warm

cold air no longer touched my body

Purpose
depends on memory   Memory

fades   moves in mystery

Oaths are straws   men guard
as they graze

herding and feeding

Snow at night   and still snowing
not a house stirring

Save for air   nothing here

7.

about the historical Arthur
about the passing of Arthur

the wild sea (his lair) War
the throwing away of Excalibur

Through secret parables through
books of dark necessity

along a line of legend winters old
we approach each other   (wordplay

of spell and spell) A listener
on the dreamer's dream depends

dreamers seeming seeing never ends

Two sisters at work under an oak
spinning and weaving   Idea

and Echo wavering só
I wish I could see them (mist)

into clear reason (air)
Music murmurs double discord

(lark and toad change eyes) Figures
metaphysical spectres

cold cold warriors   moving
and mumbling   veiled allegories

deeply veiled

Lips (keepers of thought)
whistle us off   Sound dies away

caught up in clouds to meet the air
A fictive sphere

(hawk and lark soar)
In this wide Quietness   a field

is the world I am a child   Eve
who kisses the bees   enumerates

miracles

8.

Igraine
great with child that shall be

Arthur
lying on the ground   among

sentinels
(wrapped in a military cloak)

in the gray dawn
In the grey dawn

every omen believed   (wolf
in the camp

bees in a tree) dark hyacinth
and errant ivy

Symbols are imaginary   the real
unseen (seems)

clear as far

a theme of empty air   December
harmony

icy transparency   here
we are   (Distance

and Difference   remote in time
death-pale in dream

aboriginal mother and father)

A perfect day
sweet sea-sounds in the pines

all the shores marked

Outside the window fictions are
crumbling

The being of Being is will   was
something—

and to leave without knowing it

City glittering in sunset search after
Eros

9.

Rapt away to darkness   at home in
Perilous

Helios flees secretly across a lost
country   Zodiacal sign

Sun
—this is a circle and serpent in

circle—
fit for green fable   Firmament

and it was so

Visionary events stretching back to
Eden   Thraldom

seeds to be sorted   Where
have I been I say to myself   Mother

winding as she does around the axis
How far

back through Memory   does memory

extend   a gap
in knowledge   before all people

tell
historical past   the historical

truth
a Parlance   spoken by strangers

to interpreters
Sneaping wind   a winter setting

salty sea thudding
salty sea thudding

national anthem of my love Lucifer

night so black the centuries cannot
see

10.

Each sequent separate musician
(harmony

a passion)
across a deep divided deprivation

(enchantment   captivity
a paradise-prison)

seems to hear a voice walking in the
garden

who seems to say
I am master of myself and of the

Universe

These characters observe   are known
successively withdrawn

Those passages as myth   in Myth
remain a fiction

Ever tolling absence homeward   Words
toil their way forward

a true world
fictively constructed

Boundary of day   and day
Symmetry I cannot see

Perspectives perish with ourselves

end of a house stretching its walls
away

11.

Intellect idea and (Real) being
Perpetual swipe of glaciers dividing

pearl (empyrean ocean)
Text of traces crossing   orient

and occident   Penelope
who is the image of philosophy

(your wisdom hidden in a mystery)
what ships I have seen

Sails filling   or falling
horizons wandering   real world

and yet a dream world
(immediacy) hold fast to this

Gradations of light die into distance

loose themselves in light   Darkness

Shapes   shadow-hunting
Supremacy

(now a cast shadow)
Height of that tower diminished to

this letter
Light narrowed to this point or line

Forfeit feeds nativity

Ruin into rout
antiquity—   Runes

a row of signs
ordering sound

(sacred and secret tree systems)
I sleep

or half sleep   Selflessness
and skylark   swallowed up

Mountains and summer move   Snow
includes them

green syllables of scenery in spring

12.

To trip a careless runner's crown
War

approaches its abstract form   Play
of possibilities

probabilities

(mechanical necessitarianism)

good and bad luck
Voracious coinage at the confines

political acres of prey and chirrup
Confusion

of lines bisecting   shred
after shred   of feeling

Cleared up cold this morning
Foraging

and straggling
To see through all things clearly

is to see through all things dimly
Marches

and maneuvers
Incessantly advancing towards the aim of

standing still

13.

One generation falling asleep

another waking up   Memory
harmony   multiplicity

sheen of sacramental mystery

intellection of fate and fame
unfathomable visionary dream

Knowledge is simple recollection

Recollection returns
forgotten   Boundless

time   inattention
Finite velocity

it has happened   it is history
Tracing

the change in ideas about change

Drafts

of furiously scrambled pages Scraps
of beginnings

and the problem of lost Originals
Approach to the Castle of Perilous

knight tested by the illusion

of nothingness   Estray
into my own Exile

(a dome to hive) Majestical
Soul is a god   and sun is a God

on the horizon   (Principle
vision)   out of an ocean

Soul is the maker of sun   She
is dressed as a man

Beholder in silence and in utter

forgetfulness

Dream of wandering in woods with

my father
Leaves are white   his dress

is white
(considered as white)

cut as if carved in marble   Pure
outline of form

fading from color and from frame

We look into distance as a dream
what we are

and we are not   Threading mazes

of unwearied thought

Long long years
grain sprouting from body   wheat

and barley

A border-rider's kingdom
(holy horse not to be ridden

holy places not to be trodden) Wheel

of Destiny
Plato's spindle of necessity

pantheon of history shivered into

ruin
Walking about at a gate with keys

Singing the keys

Looking west with a low sun
Mystical gaiety

irrational dimensions of an infinite city

Perspectives enter

and disappear
The perpetual dead embark   Hoop

of horizon
negation pursuit and illusion

fourscore and fade

a moving doom of brood
(ideas gems games dodges

scaffolding)

Long pythagorean lustrum

nothing new can come into being
Change

and juxtaposition
(heavenly systems move monotonous

motion)
Green grows the morning

in a first college of Something
austere music

ideal republic
Language ripples our lips

Sparrows peck at the gravel
(caged words

setting them free)
Sing the golden verses of Pythagoras

(were they ever really written)
Sweet notes

deaf sea
Outside at the back of the sky

biography blows away

16.

—You are asleep Penelope
says a shadowy figure from

the Odyssey
A dream soul from Barbarous

We are alone
and we are alone   Nomads

and a loving family
where nobody nobody nobody

no matter at all

Light has made the circuit of
the Universe

Leaves shiver shrinking back
to dark

The measure of force
(as magnitude)   as fixed

in flux
Absolute magnitudes

regions untenanted by stars

Hearer and the half-articulate
nearer and nearer

the secret Secret

Clay has fallen on my monologue
Clay on my coat

cold clay on my coat

Measure a million million
measure a million to margin

Steadfast into this sliding

no sequence seen

Thales
supposed the earth to float on

water
Infinite matter

(Anaximander)
Ocellus of Luciana and his work on

the Universe

(Entelechy)
actuality of the body   Texts

torn from their context

Forms
back into names

Newton's sailor paces three miles
an hour

while the ship sails west

Doomsday overturns and milleniums

riddance and rest

Blind wisdom wanders along
(arrows for thought

left side of the world)
Sleeps very little

We hear her walking in her room
moving through measured

velocity
Passing away according to restless

necessity

Irascible unknowable disorderly
irrational

Poverty my mother and Possession

my father
Time to set our face homeward

Shadow-emperor

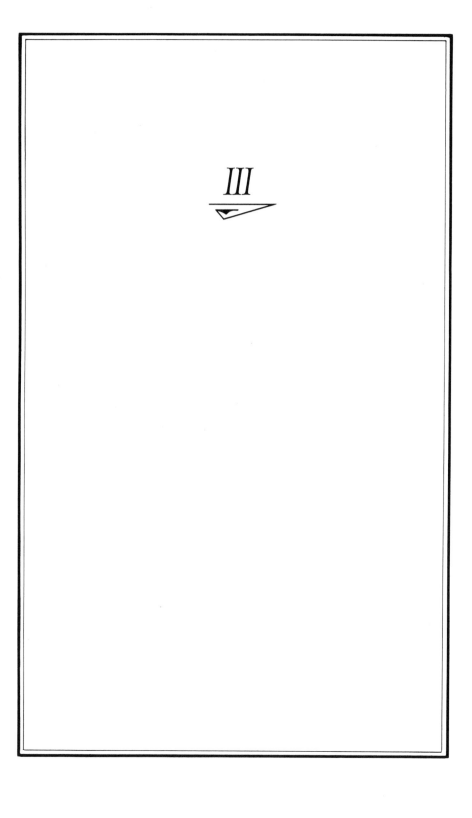

III

Some particular place   fleeting

and fixed   Particulars

fleeting and frail

Nature ties a body to my soul

Conceiving inventing falsifying

assuming

I walk through valleys stray

imagining myself free

My mind's eye   elegaic Meditation

embracing something

some history of Materialism

Orators plunge

legs doubled under them

and the Encyclopaedists

great, the Great, and GREAT

discover A.D.

in a land of pages

where the No's have it

Battles cheap as water

fought ferociously

on paper

Women and children

where are we drifting

Achilles has marched off

into pencilled Constraint

into the night of Troy

and her massacres

The flame is lit

I see the knife

deer to bleed for me

and he could kill his child

that 'happy king'

could be as stone

Stumbling over clothes the actors move

'A long way off at dusk—' one says

Nohow   a boiling sea

Vacuists cast formulas aside

as useless

Immigrant (fox-skin cap

embroidered cloak) Scholiast

O lightfoot

No spread of your name

no fabulous birth stories

no nations taken by storm

Moving in solitary symbols through shadowy

surmises

of late starlight undreamt of

interested him

says Radamanthys in the *True History*

riddles (for all his sayings) lost

Putting it differently

odd Universe and fiery envelope

'Farewell' left in a sentence

was wattling   roaming   and haze

Metaphysic or physic   seems

some clue

fox is the track   Pale

she said   I knew you knew

clear cry a cause

(no lie) hounds they race all night

w

whortleberries   haw   pied   dun

unhired   churlheart   cress

rath   lintel   stag   hazel

salmon   blackthorn   bracken   wel

peak   furze   hut

ceremony
ceremony

crop   wattling   revelry   brink

curlew

dark

a bare. . . . .

whine down hungry rang (smitten)

Little girl in your greed
come down

come down

ivy and roses   ourself
will be

without defect

without decay

only what is lovely   lies
faraway

—Day of grey clouds
and a river

no secrets spoken together
names

long as remember—

rows and rows of reeds
reeds

could be years
—The reeds of sleep

and does death end   sleep

oar   oarblades

        many-hued

clove her to be births

        lapping

or surges

        stone men gazing

soil of earth

        fair tangled trees

through a forest glade

        she fled

hazel wand

        a deer again

no mother

        but a gentle doe

chased by white hounds

        across summer sands

lapped by ripples

        of a summer sea

Spinners and spinsters

riddles engulf

cobwebs mimic rings in rain

(chains)   muddy and melodious

Quince has come here to crouch

as cock   kite   rook   roe   raven

Set work on wheels   (shadow

on shadow)

can spin more false than fair

can spin more false than fair

bat   eunuch   light   ring   run

faun   clamor   thraldom

humanchild
humanchild

stratagem   fleece   sort   seed

diadem

winnow   welter   brine   feign

wasp   goat   frog   vulture   stork   ant

nightingale   grammarian

Flora(of secrecy) specter

goat-skin

seeds

ancientry   yoke   thraldom

desert   wolv   shepherd   rill   raven

timid   satyr   vesper   winnow

    snow   chastity   berry-blood (secrecy)

rosemary   poplar   holm-oak   juniper

holly   casket   cud

wicket-gate
wicket-gate

cherubim   golden   swallow

amulet   instruction   tribulation

winged   joy   parent   sackcloth   ash

den   sealed   ascent   flee

chariot   interpret   flame

hot   arc   chaff   meridian

in the extant manuscript SOMEONE
has lightly scored a pen over

diadem   dagger   a voyage   gibbet

sheaf

weeds shiver and my clothes spread wide